Contents

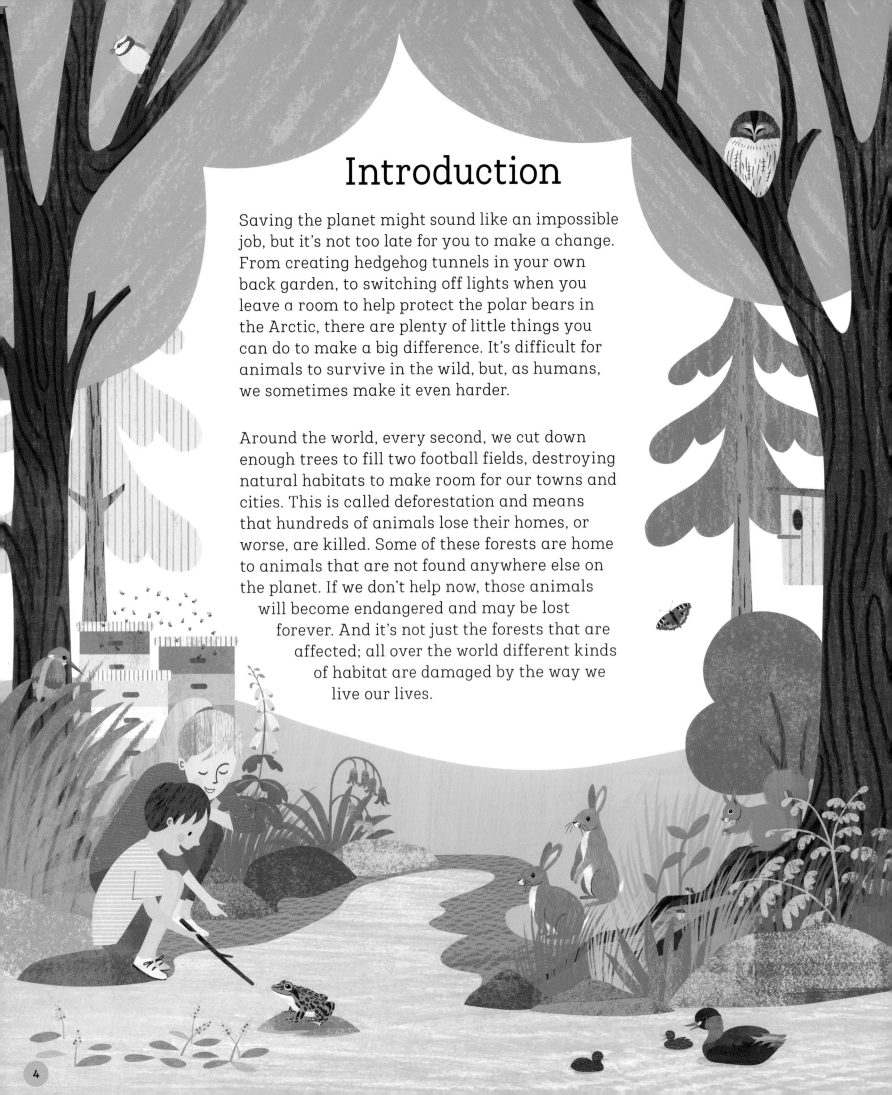

Introduction

Saving the planet might sound like an impossible job, but it's not too late for you to make a change. From creating hedgehog tunnels in your own back garden, to switching off lights when you leave a room to help protect the polar bears in the Arctic, there are plenty of little things you can do to make a big difference. It's difficult for animals to survive in the wild, but, as humans, we sometimes make it even harder.

Around the world, every second, we cut down enough trees to fill two football fields, destroying natural habitats to make room for our towns and cities. This is called deforestation and means that hundreds of animals lose their homes, or worse, are killed. Some of these forests are home to animals that are not found anywhere else on the planet. If we don't help now, those animals will become endangered and may be lost forever. And it's not just the forests that are affected; all over the world different kinds of habitat are damaged by the way we live our lives.

But don't worry, we know more now about how to protect our planet than we ever have done before. We're constantly discovering new ways to be more environmentally friendly and this will help make things better for the future. Even on a small scale, there are many things you can do to help save the world's most endangered animals and their habitats.

Taking care of nature is not just important, it's really fun too! So, what are you waiting for? Get outside, explore, and read on to discover how YOU can help protect our planet . . .

What is a habitat?

A habitat is a home for nature. Here are some of the major habitats in the world, all rich with wildlife.

GARDENS

A **garden** is an outside space near a house, which is part of a human home. Gardens often have pretty flowers and areas of green grass. Although gardens are not created naturally, they are still very important to wildlife.

HEDGEROWS

Hedgerows are long, thin stretches of bushy plants that were originally used by farmers to separate different fields. They are usually made up of woody shrubs, small trees and beautiful flowering plants. Some hedgerows contain prickly plants, like hawthorn, to stop sheep and cattle from leaving their fields.

HEATHLANDS

Heathlands are one of the rarest habitats in the world. They are wide, open spaces covered in low-lying plants, such as heather, grasses and gorse. They are usually found in places with very sandy or acidic soil. With their open areas for basking in the sun and healthy populations of insects, heathlands are just the right home for amphibians and reptiles.

WOODLANDS

Woodlands are areas of land that are covered by trees. Many are ancient habitats, and some trees are hundreds of years old! Woodland floors are littered with dead leaves and rotting wood, which makes a perfect environment for fungi, insects and shade-loving flowers.

HIGHLANDS

The Scottish **highlands** are made up of mountains, lochs and glens. 'Loch' is the Gaelic word for lake. The most famous loch is Loch Ness, where many people believe a monster called Nessie lives! A glen is a deep, narrow valley, which was carved by glaciers thousands of years ago during the last ice age.

WETLANDS

Wetlands are areas that are covered in water for all or most of the year. They are often created by flooding. Swamps, bogs, fens, marshes, mudflats and mangroves are all examples of wetlands.

FRESHWATER

Freshwater is water that contains very little salt. It is found in ponds, rivers, lakes and glaciers. Freshwater is much more rare than saltwater and it makes up less than three per cent of Earth's water!

COASTLINES

The **coastline** is the area where the land meets the sea. There are many different habitats along the coast, including beaches, sand dunes, estuaries and cliffs. All of these are salty, wet and home to lots of amazing animals.

OCEANS

Seas and **oceans** are enormous areas of saltwater. Over 70 per cent of the Earth's surface is covered by seas and oceans, making them the largest ecosystem in the world. They have the greatest variety of life, from enormous whales to tiny plankton, and from coral reefs in the warm tropics to polar bears in the freezing Arctic.

SAVANNAHS

Savannahs are huge, flat plains covered in long grasses and dotted with trees. They are usually found between rainforests and deserts. Savannahs are difficult environments to live in, so savannah animals depend upon one another to stay alive.

JUNGLES

Jungles are areas that are densely covered with trees and thick with tangled vegetation. They are usually found in tropical areas such as the Amazon in South America, the Daintree in Australia and the Congo in Africa. They are often wet and humid.

MOUNTAINS

A **mountain** is an area of land that reaches much higher than all of the land around it. It often has steep, rocky sides. Mountains are tough places to live, as there is not much food and it can be very cold. The higher you go up a mountain, the colder it gets!

Gardens

House sparrow

Garden tiger moth

Gardens are home to a lot of wild animals, including butterflies, hedgehogs, birds and even frogs and toads! As more and more houses are built, gardens are getting smaller and smaller.

Hedgehog

Small tortoiseshell
butterfly

Slow-worm

These smaller gardens often have sturdy fences, or even walls, put up to separate them from their neighbours. This means animals like hedgehogs cannot pass freely from one garden to another, making it difficult for them to find food, water and mates.

Garden species fact file

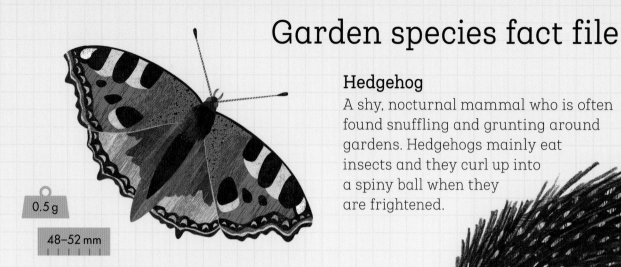

Hedgehog

A shy, nocturnal mammal who is often found snuffling and grunting around gardens. Hedgehogs mainly eat insects and they curl up into a spiny ball when they are frightened.

600 g

20–30 cm

Hedgehogs have been around for 15 million years!

0.5 g

48–52 mm

Small tortoiseshell butterfly

One of the first butterflies to appear in spring and often found hibernating in outbuildings over the winter months. Its caterpillars feed on stinging nettles.

How you can help

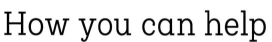 Plant native flowers with lots of nectar for bees and butterflies to visit.

Bees can see purple flowers more clearly than any other colour, whilst butterflies love them all!

Garden tiger moth

A big, brightly-coloured moth, whose markings warn that it is poisonous to predators. Its caterpillars are known as 'woolly bears' because they are very hairy!

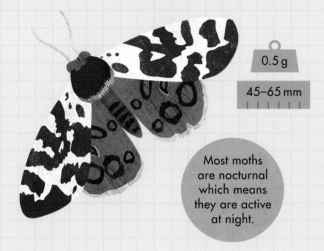

0.5 g

45–65 mm

Most moths are nocturnal which means they are active at night.

House sparrow

A small, brown bird with a dome-shaped skull. It has lived alongside humans for thousands of years and is often spotted nesting in the walls of buildings.

14–18 cm

24–40 g

Slow-worm

Often mistaken for a snake, it is actually a lizard with no legs! It likes to burrow and can usually be found hiding under rocks and logs.

100 g

Up to 50 cm

Build up any steep edges with stones or pebbles to help animals crawl out.

 Don't put down slug pellets – they can kill hedgehogs and other garden animals.

Cut a tunnel in your fence so hedgehogs can pass through your garden on their nightly food hunts.

 If you have a pond in your garden, make sure there is a gentle slope so any creatures that fall in can easily escape.

 Collect rainwater in a large container, such as a water butt, and use that to water the plants in your garden.

Hedgerows

Cuckoo

Hedgerows are perfect homes for nectar-loving insects such as butterflies and moths and for farmland birds, dormice and hedgehogs, which nest in their dense leaves. Hedgerows make wildlife corridors, allowing animals to move safely from one place to another. They can also stop soil erosion and store carbon, which helps to combat climate change.

Hazel dormouse

Stag beetle

Turtle dove

Common lizard

Hedgerows are being cut down to make bigger fields, to be replaced with fences and to make space to build houses and other buildings. They are also threatened by the use of chemicals such as pesticides and fertilisers – bad news for all the animals that live here.

Hedgerow species fact file

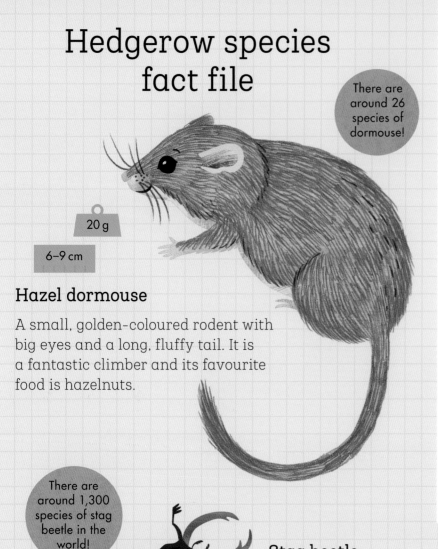

There are around 26 species of dormouse!

20 g

6–9 cm

Hazel dormouse

A small, golden-coloured rodent with big eyes and a long, fluffy tail. It is a fantastic climber and its favourite food is hazelnuts.

 Attach nestboxes to trees for hazel dormice to snuggle up in during the day.

Unlike bird boxes, dormouse nestboxes have entrance holes facing the tree which reduces the chances that birds will try to use the box too.

There are around 1,300 species of stag beetle in the world!

Stag beetle

The adult male uses its big, antler-like jaws for fighting. Its young, called 'beetle grubs', live in old trees and rotting wood. They can take up to seven years to become adults.

5 cm   3 g

24–29 cm

130 g

Turtle dove

A small and dainty bird, best known for the soft purring noise it makes. It migrates to Africa in the winter months to escape the cold.

Cuckoo

A loud, grey bird with a stripy chest. It tricks other birds into raising its chicks by laying its eggs in their nests. Cheeky cuckoos!

110 g

32–34 cm

Some lizards drop off their tails if they are caught by predators.

10–16 cm

5 g

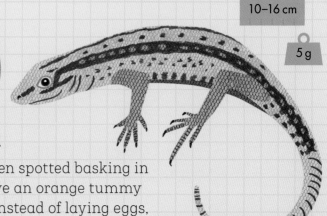

Common lizard

A brown lizard often spotted basking in the sun. Males have an orange tummy with black spots. Instead of laying eggs, the females give birth to live babies.

How you can help

 Take part in online nature surveys with the People's Trust for Endangered Species. In the 'Great Stag Hunt' you can look for stag beetles and record your sightings.

 Have fun exploring your local hedgerows to see what species you can spot. Perhaps there might be a chance for you and your family to grow a wildlife-friendly hedge in your own garden.

Do what you can to spread the word at school. You could set up a club to care for local habitats or even invite an expert to teach you more about your favourite species.

 Leave out piles of logs so lizards can hibernate under them to stay warm and survive through the winter months.

A roof will keep everything dry!

Hollow stems, like bamboo canes, or holes drilled into wood, make good hiding spots for bees and ladybirds

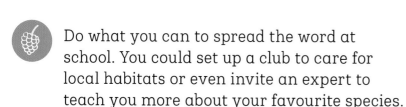

Build insect hotels out of recycled wood to put in your local hedgerows.

Beetles, spiders and woodlice all love to hide between pine cones and twigs.

Heathlands

Heathlands support many rare species, such as the Dartford warbler, the nightjar, the woodlark and the ladybird spider. All six of the UK's reptile species can be found in heathlands.

Skylark

European hare

Wart-biter cricket

When new sites are targeted for development, heathland is often top of the list, as its dry soil has few nutrients and means it is no use to farmers. Over the last one hundred years, the UK has lost half of its heathland habitats.

Smooth snake

Shrill carder bumblebee

Heathland species fact file

European hare

A lightning-fast member of the rabbit family, it has long legs and black-tipped ears. It can often be seen bounding across fields in a zigzag pattern.

45–65 cm

3–4 kg

Shrill carder bumblebee

One of the smallest and rarest bumblebees, with dark stripes on a greyish-green body. When it flies it makes a very high-pitched buzz. Bees help pollinate crops so fewer bees is bad news for all of us.

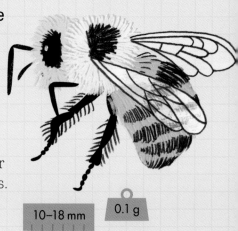

10–18 mm

0.1 g

Smooth snake

A grey-brown, spotted snake with a slender body and a small head. Very secretive and well camouflaged in heathland, it is mainly found in dry and sandy sites.

90–150 g

50–60 cm

Skylark

A streaky brown bird with a tuft of feathers on top of its head, known for its beautiful song. When the male sings, it flies straight up in the air, high into the sky.

Birds can eat 80 per cent of their own body weight in one day!

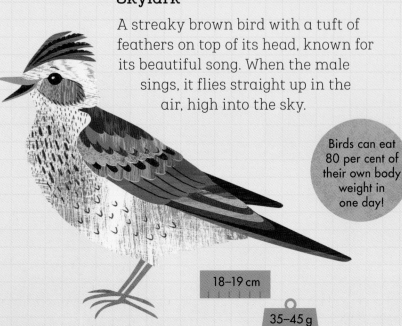

18–19 cm

35–45 g

Crickets are in the same family as grasshoppers.

31–37 mm

0.5 g

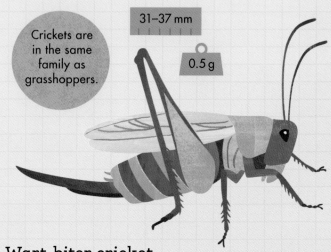

Wart-biter cricket

A large, green bush cricket with powerful back legs. It makes a clicking sound by rubbing its wings together. In the 1700s, people used them to bite warts off their skin!

How you can help

If it's not far, don't use the car. More cars means more air pollution, which is unhealthy for animals and people.

Keep dogs on a lead when you are walking in heathlands so that they don't scare birds that nest on the ground.

Buy recycled paper and wood products, such as toilet roll, to save cutting down trees in heathland areas.

Ask your grown-ups not to use chemical pesticides or fertilisers on flowers as these can kill bees.

Pack a no-rubbish lunch. If rubbish is left on the ground or blows away, it can be really harmful to wildlife if they swallow it or get stuck in it.

About one third of all the rubbish we throw away is packaging, so use a lunchbox with dividers to keep your food fresh instead.

Choose a reusable bottle for your drinks.

Woodlands

Barbastelle bat

Red squirrel

Cicada

Woods and trees are home to more wildlife than any other habitat – and they have been around for thousands of years. Woodlands are especially important for beetles, woodland birds, mosses, ferns and lichens. Many mammals also depend on woodlands for food and places to hide.

Cosnard's
net-winged
beetle

Blue ground
beetle

Woodlands are rapidly shrinking
in size. They are threatened by
pollution, pests, disease and clearing
for new developments. Trees are
cut down to make space for new
housing, train lines and farmland.

Woodland species fact file

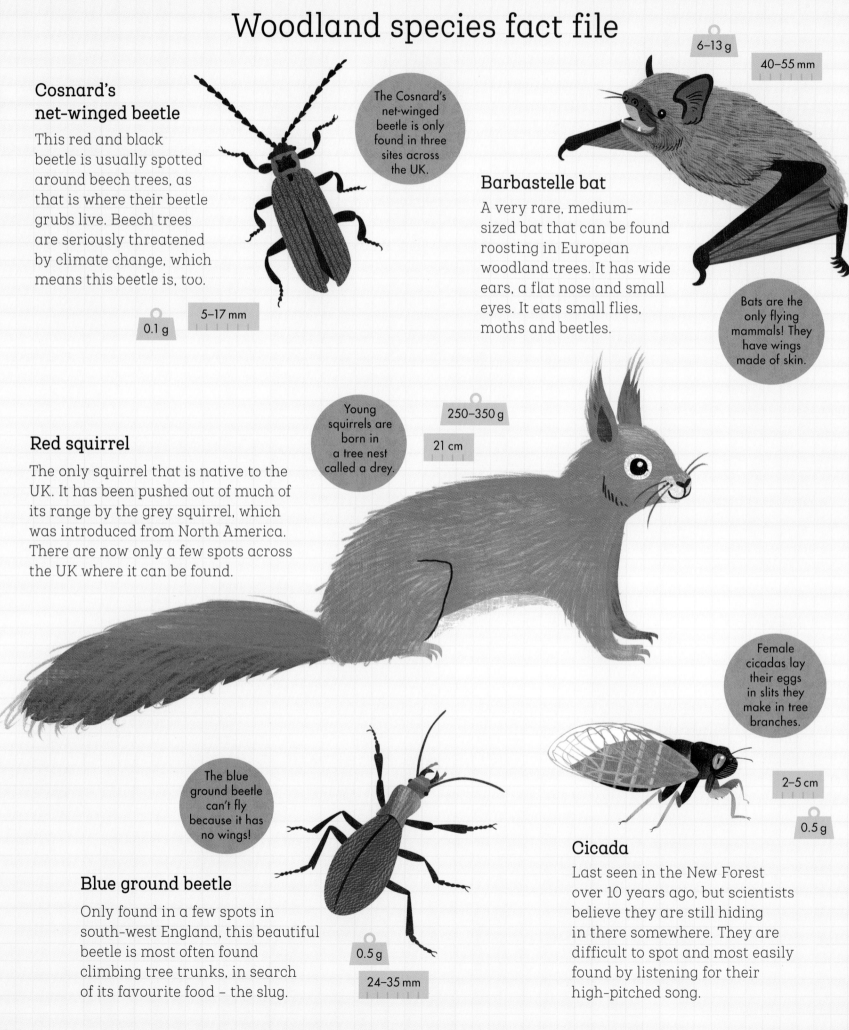

Cosnard's net-winged beetle

This red and black beetle is usually spotted around beech trees, as that is where their beetle grubs live. Beech trees are seriously threatened by climate change, which means this beetle is, too.

The Cosnard's net-winged beetle is only found in three sites across the UK.

0.1 g

5–17 mm

Barbastelle bat

A very rare, medium-sized bat that can be found roosting in European woodland trees. It has wide ears, a flat nose and small eyes. It eats small flies, moths and beetles.

6–13 g

40–55 mm

Bats are the only flying mammals! They have wings made of skin.

Red squirrel

The only squirrel that is native to the UK. It has been pushed out of much of its range by the grey squirrel, which was introduced from North America. There are now only a few spots across the UK where it can be found.

Young squirrels are born in a tree nest called a drey.

250–350 g

21 cm

Female cicadas lay their eggs in slits they make in tree branches.

The blue ground beetle can't fly because it has no wings!

2–5 cm

0.5 g

Blue ground beetle

Only found in a few spots in south-west England, this beautiful beetle is most often found climbing tree trunks, in search of its favourite food – the slug.

0.5 g

24–35 mm

Cicada

Last seen in the New Forest over 10 years ago, but scientists believe they are still hiding in there somewhere. They are difficult to spot and most easily found by listening for their high-pitched song.

How you can help

 Trees provide a warm and cosy habitat for tiny insects so don't pull bark or branches off of them.

 A log pile makes a wonderful habitat for all sorts of creatures so if you disturb one, don't forget to put it back how you found it.

 Adopt a red squirrel from The Wildlife Trust. By donating money each month, you can stop them from dying out.

During the winter, many insects stay warm and cosy under logs.

 Save paper by using the same piece on both sides. The less paper you use, the less trees will need to be chopped down.

 Download apps that help you monitor wildlife, such as the New Forest Cicada app which helps you search for cicadas if you're visiting the New Forest.

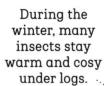 Visit your local woodlands to learn about the species that live there. Search online to find accessible routes for wheelchairs, pushchairs and mobility aids.

Highlands

The Highlands are home for dragonflies and damselflies, which are common around the lochs. Red deer, beavers and eagles can also be found in the moors, rivers and skies.

Western capercaillie

Tiger worm

Golden eagle

Scottish wildcat

Climate change is one of the biggest threats to the Scottish highlands. A change in temperature and rainfall may mean that some highland species are no longer able to survive. It will also encourage new species to spread to the area, bringing diseases that could kill highland animals.

Highlands species fact file

80–90 cm

4–8 kg

The wildcat looks like a domestic cat, but is bigger and has a shorter, thicker tail.

Scottish wildcat

Once found all over the UK, they are now very rare and only found in certain sites in Scotland. There are probably less than 100 left in the wild.

Start noticing more in nature. Take photos, paint pictures or write a story about the animals you find when you explore outside.

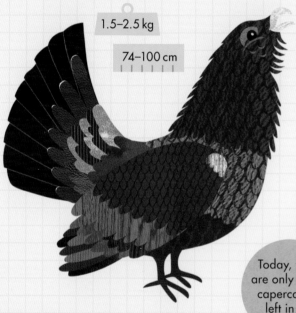

1.5–2.5 kg

74–100 cm

Western capercaillie

A large bird that spends most of its time on the ground where it feeds on berries, insects and grasses. During the mating season the males perform impressive mating displays.

Today, there are only 1,200 capercaillies left in the wild.

70–84 cm

3.5–5 kg

The golden eagle can dive at over 150 miles per hour!

Tiger worm

A stripy worm that lives in leaf litter and compost heaps. It is an excellent composter and can eat its own weight in decaying vegetation in one day.

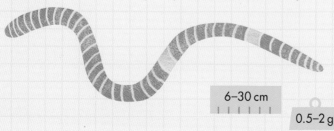

6–30 cm

0.5–2 g

Golden eagle

An enormous bird of prey that loves to glide on currents of hot air whilst searching for birds and small mammals to eat. Its nests, called 'eyries', are found in trees and on rocky cliff faces.

How you can help

Trees can take hundreds of years to become fully-grown and can live for thousands more!

 Create a new habitat for wildlife by planting native trees with your family.

 Talk to your parents about using reusable batteries. Batteries contain harmful chemicals and if they are thrown away, the chemicals can leak into the ground.

Eat locally sourced foods, which have not travelled lots of 'food-miles'.

 Switch off the lights when you leave a room to save electricity.

Try to dust your lightbulbs once in a while – dusty lightbulbs use more energy than clean ones.

Wetlands

Wetlands are very special ecosystems and they are home to many unique species. Reptiles, amphibians, invertebrates, mammals and birds can all be found in wetlands.

Grass snake

Norfolk hawker

Green tansy beetle

European otter

Wetlands are drained for two reasons; firstly to provide dry land for developers to build on, and secondly to provide farmers with water to use on their crops, or land for them to graze their animals on. Draining destroys the wetland habitat. For the wetlands that are left, the main threats are pollution and the introduction of foreign species like killer shrimp, which kill off native animals.

Water vole

Wetland species fact file

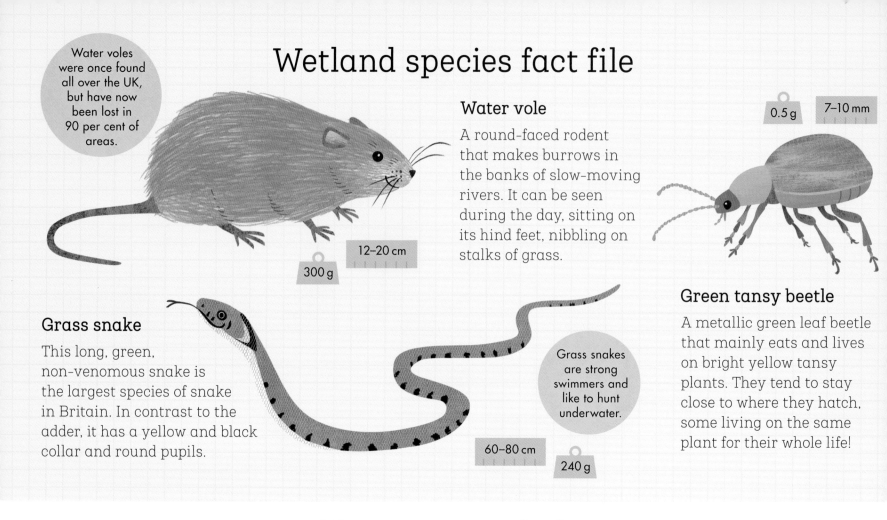

Water voles were once found all over the UK, but have now been lost in 90 per cent of areas.

Water vole

A round-faced rodent that makes burrows in the banks of slow-moving rivers. It can be seen during the day, sitting on its hind feet, nibbling on stalks of grass.

12–20 cm

300 g

0.5 g   7–10 mm

Green tansy beetle

A metallic green leaf beetle that mainly eats and lives on bright yellow tansy plants. They tend to stay close to where they hatch, some living on the same plant for their whole life!

Grass snake

This long, green, non-venomous snake is the largest species of snake in Britain. In contrast to the adder, it has a yellow and black collar and round pupils.

Grass snakes are strong swimmers and like to hunt underwater.

60–80 cm

240 g

How you can help

Stay on tracks and paths so you don't disturb nests on the ground.

Birds build nests to provide a safe place for eggs and young birds to grow.

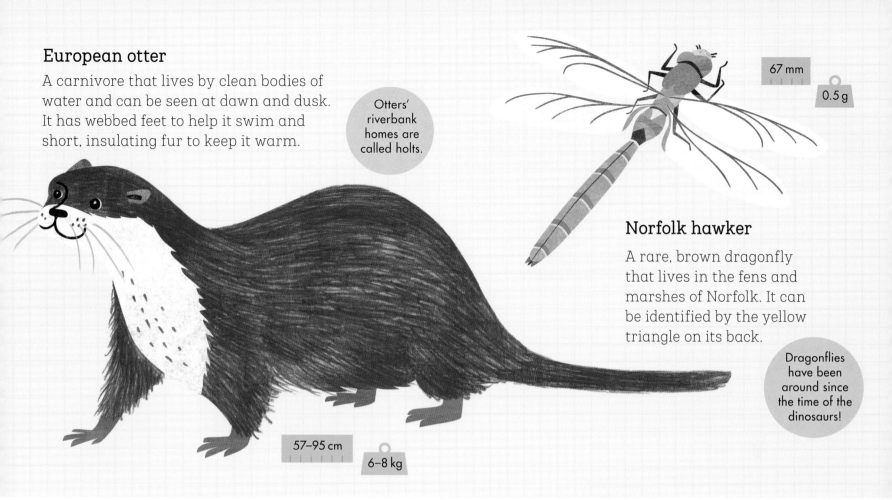

European otter

A carnivore that lives by clean bodies of water and can be seen at dawn and dusk. It has webbed feet to help it swim and short, insulating fur to keep it warm.

Otters' riverbank homes are called holts.

67 mm

0.5 g

Norfolk hawker

A rare, brown dragonfly that lives in the fens and marshes of Norfolk. It can be identified by the yellow triangle on its back.

Dragonflies have been around since the time of the dinosaurs!

57–95 cm

6–8 kg

Join in with riverbank restoration programs to help protect the habitat for river wildlife.

Take part in online dragonfly and butterfly counts to find out which species live in your local wetland.

Learn to identify wetland species and tell your family and friends about why they are so important.

Volunteer to monitor a local water vole population.

Water voles are Britain's fastest declining wild mammal. Look out for their burrows in the riverbank, often with nibbled grass around the entrance.

Freshwater

Much like hedgerows act as corridors for land animals, rivers and streams help freshwater species to move safely around wetland ecosystems. These bodies of freshwater are home to fish such as eels, pike and roach, mammals like water voles and otters and beautiful birds such as kingfishers.

White-clawed crayfish

Freshwater habitats suffer from pollution from many different sources. Industrial sites, sewage tanks and fish farms all pump their waste into freshwater habitats. Fertilisers that drain off farmland into freshwater can cause algae and weeds to grow too much, choking the water and killing off all other species that are living in the area.

Great crested newt

Vendace

Freshwater pearl mussel

Amazon river dolphin

Freshwater species fact file

25–50 g

20 cm

White-clawed crayfish look like miniature lobsters!

Vendace fish are now only found in a couple of lakes in the UK.

Vendace

A rare, small, silvery fish, which has been around since the last ice age and lives in deep, cold lakes. Many people thought it had already gone extinct.

90 g

12 cm

20 g

12–15 cm

White-clawed crayfish

The only species of freshwater crayfish that is native to the British Isles, it is endangered by the introduction of non-native species like the American signal crayfish.

Freshwater pearl mussels cling on to the gills of salmon when they are first born.

Freshwater pearl mussel

Large, dark brown mussels that can live for more than 100 years! They live on the bottom of riverbeds, where they filter food out of the water.

Dolphins communicate using a variety of clicks and whistles.

100–160 kg

2–3 m

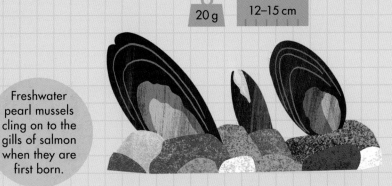

Amazon river dolphin

A mammal that lives in South American rivers. It has a long, thin snout, small eyes and a grey-pink body. It eats a variety of river fish, including ferocious piranhas.

Amphibians bask in the sun to keep warm.

6–10 g

14–16 cm

Great crested newt

A warty brown amphibian with a jagged crest along its back and a bright orange tummy. It prefers big ponds with lots of weeds and no fish.

How you can help

 Be responsible and put rubbish in the bin. If you drop it on the ground, it might be washed into a river and could harm freshwater wildlife.

 Ask your grown-up not to use chemical pesticides and fertilisers in the garden – they can run into rivers and could kill the fish.

Use biodegradable cleaning products, which will not pollute waterways such as rivers and streams.

Look for great crested newts with your friends. Any ponds that they are living in are protected by law, which means you are not allowed to disturb them or damage their habitat.

The great crested newt is one of three newts found in the British Isles, along with the smooth newt and the palmate newt. It is the biggest and least common of the three.

Coastlines

Little tern

Coasts are home to seabirds, waders, sea mammals and lots of other creatures, too. They soak up energy from the sea and help stop the risk of flooding and erosion. It is important to protect coasts, not only for animals, but for people, too.

Natterjack toad

Harbour porpoise

Puffin

The greatest threat to coastal species is the litter that is washed up by the tides. Plastic litter is often found in the stomachs of dead sea creatures, and sometimes it strangles them when it gets wrapped around their bodies. Coasts are also threatened by pollution from farming, industrial waste and sewage.

Sand lizard

Coastal species fact file

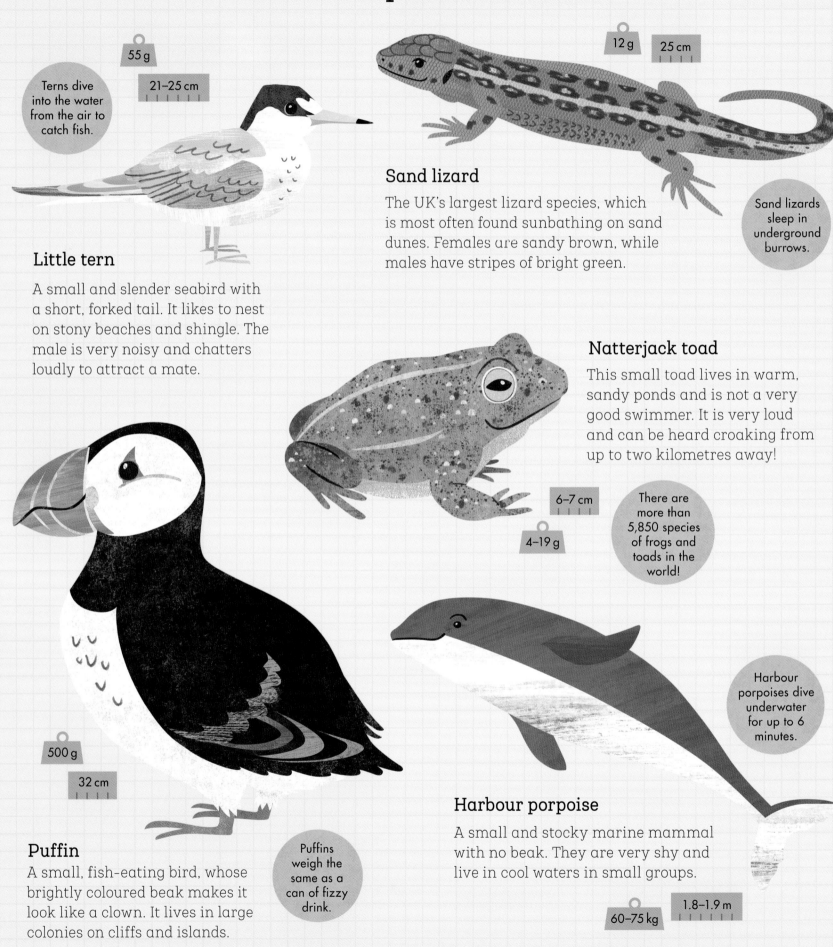

55 g

21–25 cm

Terns dive into the water from the air to catch fish.

Little tern

A small and slender seabird with a short, forked tail. It likes to nest on stony beaches and shingle. The male is very noisy and chatters loudly to attract a mate.

12 g

25 cm

Sand lizard

The UK's largest lizard species, which is most often found sunbathing on sand dunes. Females are sandy brown, while males have stripes of bright green.

Sand lizards sleep in underground burrows.

Natterjack toad

This small toad lives in warm, sandy ponds and is not a very good swimmer. It is very loud and can be heard croaking from up to two kilometres away!

6–7 cm

4–19 g

There are more than 5,850 species of frogs and toads in the world!

500 g

32 cm

Puffin

A small, fish-eating bird, whose brightly coloured beak makes it look like a clown. It lives in large colonies on cliffs and islands.

Puffins weigh the same as a can of fizzy drink.

Harbour porpoises dive underwater for up to 6 minutes.

Harbour porpoise

A small and stocky marine mammal with no beak. They are very shy and live in cool waters in small groups.

60–75 kg

1.8–1.9 m

How you can help

 Join in with a litter-pick on a local beach.

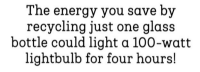 The energy you save by recycling just one glass bottle could light a 100-watt lightbulb for four hours!

 Use a reusable water bottle when you go to the beach, instead of buying a new plastic one.

 Use unbleached paper, as bleach can damage water systems.

To save water and keep our coasts healthy, don't leave the tap running when you brush your teeth.

 Pick up your dog's poo when you take it for a walk, so it doesn't spread disease.

 Don't release sky lanterns or balloons. When they land, wildlife such as coastal birds and fish can get tangled in them or choke on them.

Oceans

Oceans contain many weird and wonderful creatures, from octopuses and dolphins to seahorses and starfishes, also known as sea stars. They are also home to the largest animal in the world, the blue whale.

Leatherback
turtle

Polar bear

Blue whale

Fishing is a big problem for oceans. If too many adult fish are caught then there will be no babies to grow up into the next generation. And it is not only the fish that suffer from fishing. Animals like turtles, dolphins and whales die when they get tangled in fishing nets. This is called 'bycatch'. Our litter also causes huge problems for oceans. If things don't change, the ocean will soon contain more plastic than fish.

Atlantic
bluefin tuna

Coral

Ocean species fact file

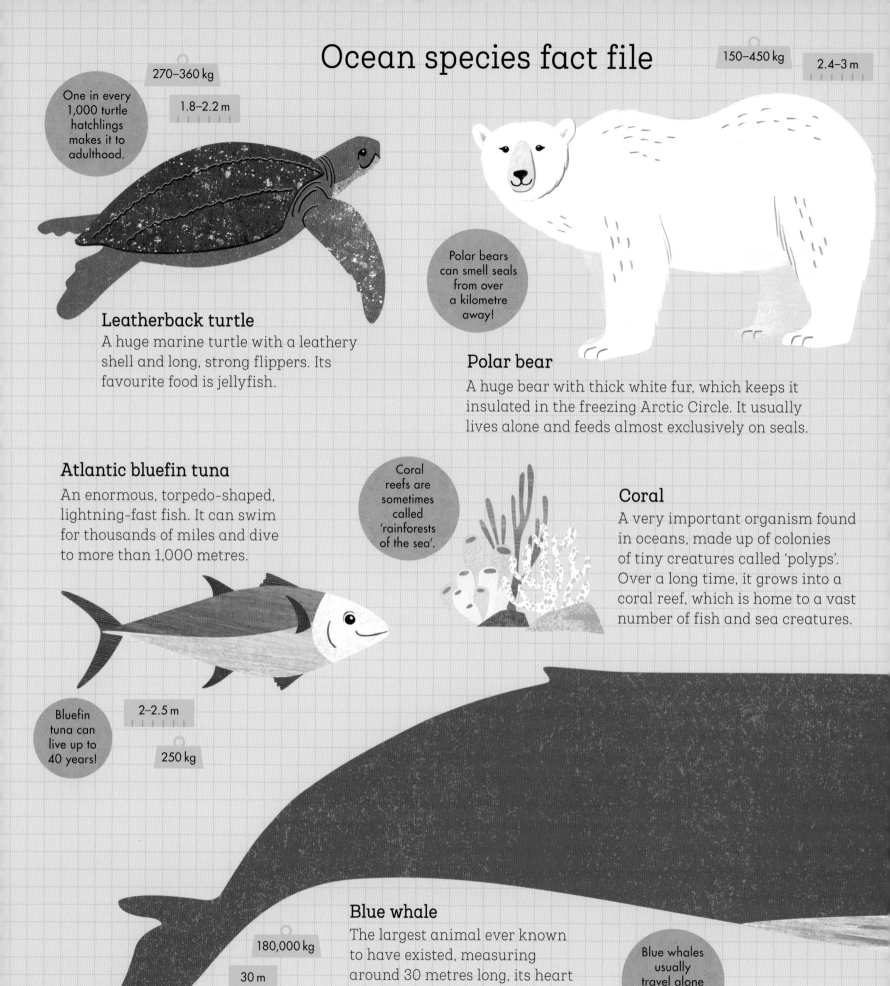

270–360 kg

1.8–2.2 m

One in every 1,000 turtle hatchlings makes it to adulthood.

150–450 kg

2.4–3 m

Leatherback turtle

A huge marine turtle with a leathery shell and long, strong flippers. Its favourite food is jellyfish.

Polar bears can smell seals from over a kilometre away!

Polar bear

A huge bear with thick white fur, which keeps it insulated in the freezing Arctic Circle. It usually lives alone and feeds almost exclusively on seals.

Atlantic bluefin tuna

An enormous, torpedo-shaped, lightning-fast fish. It can swim for thousands of miles and dive to more than 1,000 metres.

Coral reefs are sometimes called 'rainforests of the sea'.

Coral

A very important organism found in oceans, made up of colonies of tiny creatures called 'polyps'. Over a long time, it grows into a coral reef, which is home to a vast number of fish and sea creatures.

Bluefin tuna can live up to 40 years!

2–2.5 m

250 kg

180,000 kg

30 m

Blue whale

The largest animal ever known to have existed, measuring around 30 metres long, its heart is as big as a small car!

Blue whales usually travel alone or in small groups.

How you can help

 Use a reusable bag for your shopping and don't throw plastic bags into the bin. They might end up in the ocean and can become a danger to sea creatures.

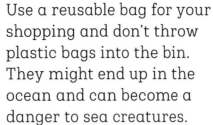 Only buy responsibly and sustainably sourced fish to eat to prevent over-fishing of endangered species.

 Don't buy wild-caught fish as pets – if we continue to take animals from the wild there will eventually be none left.

Plastic bags and other plastic rubbish thrown into the ocean kill more than one million sea creatures every year!

 Never flush wet wipes down the toilet – they don't break down like toilet paper and can harm animals in the ocean.

 Avoid using single-use plastic. Instead, use alternatives like reusable cups and cutlery or refillable bottles and jars.

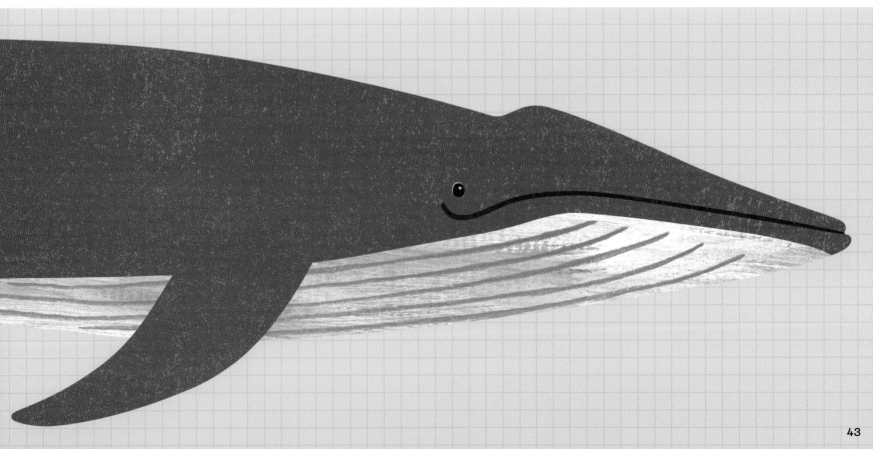

Savannahs

Rothschild's giraffe

There are savannahs all over the world. Africa's savannahs support zebras, giraffes and lions. In Australian savannahs you could find kangaroos, wallabies and echidnas. Brazil's savannahs are home to tapirs, jaguars and armadillos.

African wild dog

Ethiopian wolf

Black rhino

Deforestation and the building of mines threaten the savannah ecosystem, because there isn't enough room left for its animals who need lots of space. But the animals that live in the savannah are also targeted directly. Famous African animals are hunted and killed so that rich tourists can take their heads and skins home as trophies. Elephants are killed for their tusks, which poachers sell as ivory.

African cheetah

Savannah species fact file

900–1,350 kg

2.8–3.8 m

Rhinos can reach a speed of 30 miles per hour – as fast as a car!

Black rhino

Sometimes called the hook-lipped rhinoceros, it has a pointed upper lip, which helps it to pluck fruit and leaves from the branches of trees.

Ethiopian wolf

A canine with a long, narrow head, pointed ears, and red-and-white fur. It is a sociable animal and lives in packs. It eats rodents, such as mole rats, grass rats and hares.

There are fewer than 600 Ethiopian wolves in the wild.

84–100 cm

12–15 kg

Rothschild's giraffe

A light-coloured giraffe, which has no patches below its knees, so it looks like it's wearing long socks! Like all giraffes they have long necks, legs and tongues.

Giraffes can feed on leaves and buds at the very top of trees.

4.3–5.5 m

680–1,360 kg

Support organisations involved in savannah wildlife conservation by adopting an animal or doing a sponsored event.

ADOPT

WWF

18–27 kg

92 cm

There are around 6,600 African wild dogs left in the wild.

African wild dog

Also known as the African painted dog due to its coat, which is covered in blotches of colour. It lives and hunts in a pack, targeting large prey like antelope and wildebeest.

African cheetah

A large, spotted cat with a streamlined body, a small rounded head and powerful legs. It is the fastest land animal in the world and is very good at hunting.

112–135 cm

35–55 kg

Cheetahs can accelerate from 0–60 miles per hour in three seconds!

How you can help

Use social media to share messages about how people can help.

 Recycle old clothes and buy second-hand clothes. Making new clothes requires a lot of water and energy and the dyes and chemicals used in the process are damaging to the environment.

Never buy products made from animal parts, such as ivory. Savannah animals are poached for these products.

 Coffee crops are often grown in elephants' habitats. If you buy coffee, make sure it is elephant-friendly. Look for the certified Fairtrade Mark on the packaging.

Have a 'rhino rant' – tell your friends and family about the plight of the rhino and why we should protect it.

Jungles

Jungles are filled with incredible species. Brightly coloured birds and butterflies fill the skies, whilst monkeys and snakes swing and slither through the trees.

Orangutan

Clouded leopard

Proboscis monkey

Asian elephant

Tiger

Jungles are disappearing at a terrifying rate. They are cut down to make space to graze cattle, to use the trees for wood for building houses and furniture, and to plant crops such as palm trees to make palm oil, which is used in cooking and found in many kinds of foods.

Jungle species fact file

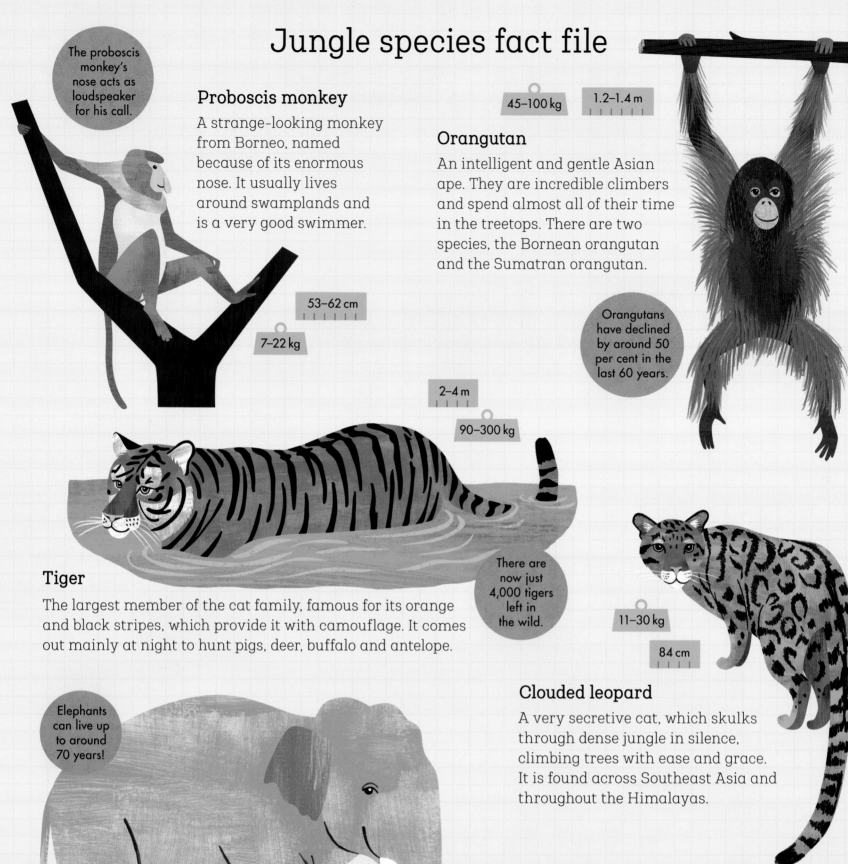

The proboscis monkey's nose acts as loudspeaker for his call.

Proboscis monkey

A strange-looking monkey from Borneo, named because of its enormous nose. It usually lives around swamplands and is a very good swimmer.

53–62 cm

7–22 kg

45–100 kg

1.2–1.4 m

Orangutan

An intelligent and gentle Asian ape. They are incredible climbers and spend almost all of their time in the treetops. There are two species, the Bornean orangutan and the Sumatran orangutan.

Orangutans have declined by around 50 per cent in the last 60 years.

2–4 m

90–300 kg

Tiger

The largest member of the cat family, famous for its orange and black stripes, which provide it with camouflage. It comes out mainly at night to hunt pigs, deer, buffalo and antelope.

There are now just 4,000 tigers left in the wild.

11–30 kg

84 cm

Clouded leopard

A very secretive cat, which skulks through dense jungle in silence, climbing trees with ease and grace. It is found across Southeast Asia and throughout the Himalayas.

Elephants can live up to around 70 years!

Asian elephant

Smaller than the African elephant, but still one of the largest land animals on the planet. It has huge ears and an amazing long trunk, which it uses for breathing, smelling, trumpeting, drinking, communicating and even picking things up!

5.5–6.5 m

2,000–4,900 kg

How you can help

Only buy products that contain sustainably sourced palm oil. To create palm oil, an area of rainforest the size of 300 football pitches has to be chopped down each hour!

'Eco' products tend to cost more, but if we all keep buying them, the prices should go down.

Put a 'No Junk Mail' sign on your door to reduce how much paper you waste.

Wear an extra layer on cold days rather than turning the heating up.

To reduce the number of jungle trees that need to be cut down, don't print things out if you don't need to.

About 40 per cent of the energy we use at home is for heat. And half of that is wasted!

Learn about which companies clear rainforests to make their products and avoid buying from them. Only buy wood that is certified by the FSC. This means it has been grown from a well-managed forest.

PALM OIL FREE

PALM OIL FREE

Mountains

Red panda

Mountain gorilla

Mountain species often have thick, woolly coats to keep them warm. Some mountain animals have specially designed feet, to keep their balance on the rocky mountainsides. Even the plants in mountain areas are specially adapted to keep them out of the wind.

Chinchilla

When new mountain roads are built, they allow loggers, poachers and miners to travel to areas that are normally very difficult to get to. New roads can also cause erosion to the steep mountain edges. Some mountain habitats are also being destroyed by the human wars that are taking place on their slopes.

Snow leopard

Mountain species fact file

90–180 kg

1.2–1.8 m

There are only around 880 mountain gorillas left in the wild.

4–6.5 kg

58 cm

Red panda

A cat-sized mammal that is more closely related to weasels and raccoons than the black and white giant panda. It lives in mountainous forests and feeds mainly on bamboo, eggs, flowers and berries.

Red pandas communicate by making a twittering sound.

Mountain gorilla

An enormous black ape with long, shaggy hair that is closely related to humans. They live in groups of many females and young with one adult male, called the silverback.

Chinchillas usually live in herds of 100 or more.

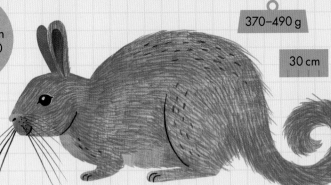

370–490 g

30 cm

Snow leopards have long furry tails that help them to balance.

Chinchilla

A South American rodent with soft and silky fur and a long, bushy tail. Found in the Andes mountain range of Chile and hunted for its fur.

Snow leopard

One of the most mysterious cats in the world, it lives in the remote mountains of Central Asia. Even its big feet are covered in thick hair to keep them warm.

1.1 m

27–55 kg

How you can help

 If something breaks, instead of buying something new, which will require materials and energy – learn how to fix it.

Make your own eco-friendly party decorations instead of using balloons to reduce plastic waste.

Create flyers to share with neighbours telling them how they can help, too.

 Use energy-efficient light bulbs as they use much less electricity than conventional bulbs.

 Make sure your flyers are made from recycled paper.

 Reuse envelopes when you can to stop so many mountain trees being chopped down.

 Never buy products made of real animal fur. Many mountain animals are killed just for their fur.

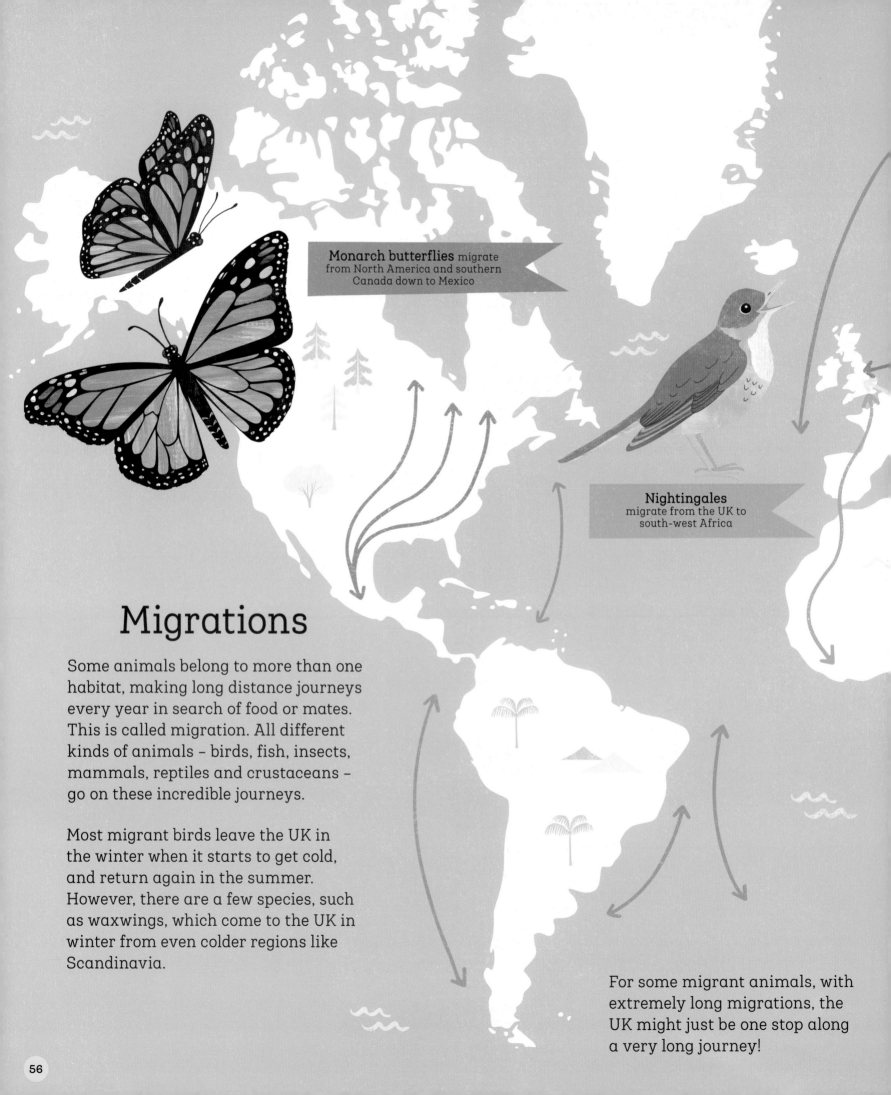

Monarch butterflies migrate from North America and southern Canada down to Mexico

Nightingales migrate from the UK to south-west Africa

Migrations

Some animals belong to more than one habitat, making long distance journeys every year in search of food or mates. This is called migration. All different kinds of animals – birds, fish, insects, mammals, reptiles and crustaceans – go on these incredible journeys.

Most migrant birds leave the UK in the winter when it starts to get cold, and return again in the summer. However, there are a few species, such as waxwings, which come to the UK in winter from even colder regions like Scandinavia.

For some migrant animals, with extremely long migrations, the UK might just be one stop along a very long journey!

Lapwings migrate from Scandinavia to the UK

Golden orioles migrate from Africa and Western Asia to the UK

Humpback whales migrate from polar waters to tropical waters

Climate change affects the plants that grow in different areas. This means that some migrant species arrive at their destinations expecting to find lots of food to eat – but nothing is there! Changing temperatures also confuse birds about when they should leave. Oil spills are another big problem for birds that have stopovers in contaminated areas along their journeys. Some migrants are even trapped by poachers or shot by hunters as they fly by.

Migrant species fact file

0.5 g 9–11 cm

Monarch butterfly

A beautiful North American butterfly that travels up to 3,000 miles to find somewhere warm to roost over the winter. They use the same roosting spots every year!

The monarch butterfly's wingspan is around 6–15 cm long.

Golden oriole

A brightly coloured but secretive bird that lives in the high canopy. It migrates to the UK in early summer to escape the hot summers of Africa and Western Asia.

56–79 g 20–24 cm

Nightingale

The noise made by this summer migrant is often described as one of the most beautiful sounds in nature. Their rich song can be heard at any time of the day or night.

15–16 cm 20 g

300 g 28–33 cm

Lapwing

These crested birds are partial migrants. Some of them migrate short distances if the weather gets very cold, while others remain near to their nesting grounds.

Humpback whales eat almost 1.5 tons of krill every day!

14–19 m 30,000 kg

Humpback whale

A large whale with a bumpy snout and very large flippers, which it uses to swim and steer. It is very noisy and sings to communicate. It jumps out of the water and dives back in – this is called 'breaching'.

How you can help

Attach window stickers to clear windows to stop birds accidentally flying into them.

If you see a baby bird on the ground, leave it alone. It's likely that its mummy will be nearby.

Put a bell on the collar of your cat so that it can't sneak up on birds.

Put food and water out for the birds, especially in winter.

Look out for wildlife campaigns and support the ones that matter to you, like The Big Garden Birdwatch by the RSPB.

Although bread is not harmful to birds, it doesn't provide many nutrients and can choke small chicks. Instead, put out chopped nuts in winter, and seeds and dried fruit in the summer.

Grow plants with berries for birds to eat.

Go birdwatching with friends and log all the different birds you can spot.

More about endangered species

So far, scientists have estimated that there are around 1.5 million different types of animal in the world, but there are likely to be many more. They are divided into six different groups and here are the approximate numbers of species for each one:

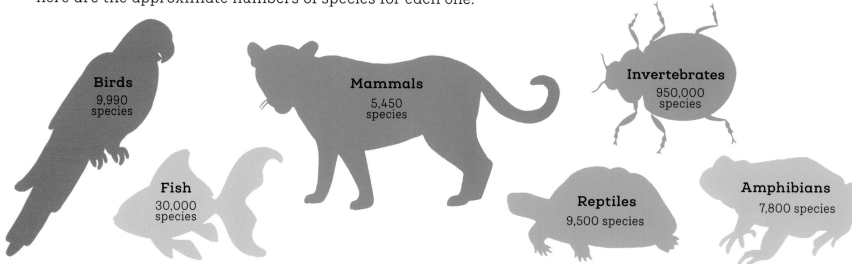

Birds
9,990 species

Fish
30,000 species

Mammals
5,450 species

Invertebrates
950,000 species

Reptiles
9,500 species

Amphibians
7,800 species

The IUCN (International Union for Conservation of Nature) is the world's main organisation for the conservation of animals from around the planet. They put together lists of animals, called Red Lists, which show the threatened status of species within a certain country or region. The endangered species are grouped into seven different categories, which show the risk that they will become extinct if we do not try to protect them. You can find out more and even look up the status of your favourite animal on their website: *www.iucnredlist.org*

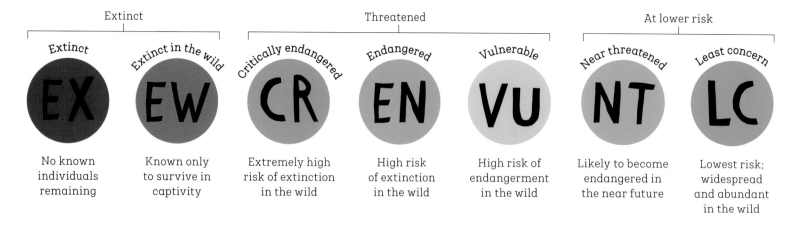

Extinct

Threatened

At lower risk

Extinct	Extinct in the wild	Critically endangered	Endangered	Vulnerable	Near threatened	Least concern
EX	**EW**	**CR**	**EN**	**VU**	**NT**	**LC**
No known individuals remaining	Known only to survive in captivity	Extremely high risk of extinction in the wild	High risk of extinction in the wild	High risk of endangerment in the wild	Likely to become endangered in the near future	Lowest risk; widespread and abundant in the wild

It is not only animals which can become endangered. There are six main habitats which are essential to life on our planet as they provide food, water, shelter and even the oxygen we breathe. All of these habitats are threatened by human actions, too.

Rainforest   Marine   Forest   Grassland   Desert   Polar

← Most animal species live here.

Least animal species live here. →

Although rainforests cover only a small part of the Earth, they're home to over half the world's plants and animals.

One and a half acres of rainforest are lost every second.

Rainforests once covered 14 per cent of the Earth's land surface.

Now they only cover 6 per cent.

Experts estimate that the last remaining rainforests could be destroyed in less than 40 years.

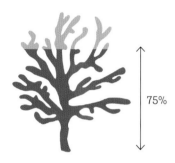

75%

Coral reefs are home to one quarter of the world's fish species and they protect the coastlines of 109 countries. But approximately 75 per cent of the world's coral reefs are rated as threatened.

About 50 per cent of all turtle species are threatened with extinction.

50%

Out of the six animal groups, amphibians are the most endangered. But, according to the IUCN, a number of species from every group are considered threatened too. Here are some approximate figures:

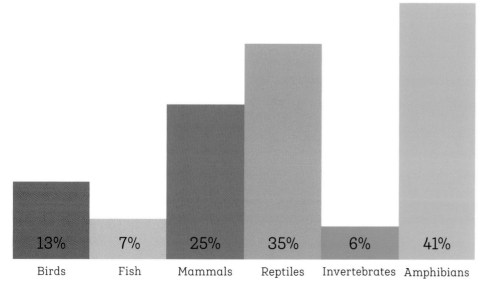

Birds	Fish	Mammals	Reptiles	Invertebrates	Amphibians
13%	7%	25%	35%	6%	41%

% of threatened species in each animal group

Going, going… gone

If we aren't careful, then animals that are endangered now will soon become extinct, like these amazing creatures who have already disappeared:

Dodo

Woolly mammoth

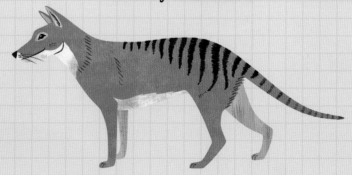

Tasmanian tiger

… and many, many more like the Pyrenean ibex, the passenger pigeon, the quagga, the Caribbean monk seal and the great auk.

More ways to help

Our beautiful planet is in danger. If we do not act soon, we will all be fighting for survival. But don't despair! If we are kind to the environment, it will give us everything we need for happy, healthy lives. We can change the future. We can save the planet. And the power to do it is in YOUR hands.

SAVE ENERGY

Only use things that run on electricity when you really need to and turn them off when you are finished. Using electricity burns up fossil fuels such as oil and coal, which is poisonous to the atmosphere.

RECYCLE

Recycle as much as you can! Cans, bottles, paper, cardboard, plastic and glass can all be turned into brand new products if they are recycled.

SPEAK OUT

Tell everyone you meet about the problems facing our planet and how we can fix them. We will all need to work together to solve the problems we have created.

SAVE WATER

Turn off the tap when you are not using the water. Creating clean drinking water uses lots of energy and produces pollution.

REUSE

Use things more than once! Before you throw something away, ask yourself how you could use it again.

REDUCE

Think before you buy! Reduce the amount of waste you produce by buying less in the first place. Also avoid buying things with lots of packaging.

PESTER POWER

Grown-ups often make most of the decisions about what to buy from the shops. Use your pester power to remind them to look for products that are friendly to the environment and don't have lots of packaging.

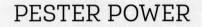

Glossary

Amphibian   A cold-blooded animal with a backbone, such as a newt or toad. Amphibians start their life with gills and a tail.

Camouflage   The way that an animal's colour or markings help it to blend in with its surroundings.

Climate change   A change in the Earth's temperature.

Compost   A rich soil made from dead plants and vegetables.

Conservation   Protecting animals, plants and the environment.

Deforestation   Clearing an area of trees.

Ecosystem   All of the plants and animals found in a certain area.

Environment   Everything around us including air, water, rocks and plants.

Erosion   The wearing away of soil and rock.

Extinct   When there are no more of a species left alive.

Fertiliser   A chemical or natural substance added to soil to make plants grow better.

Glacier   Thick ice that moves slowly downhill.

Habitat   The place where an animal or plant lives.

Hibernation   Sleeping through the cold winter months.

Industrial waste   Waste produced by places where humans work, such as factories.

Invertebrate   An animal without a backbone.

Mammal   A warm-blooded animal with a skeleton and fur or hair on its skin. Mammal mothers produce milk to feed their babies.

Mating   The way animals make babies.

Migration   Moving from one place to another, usually at a certain time of year.

Native   Belonging to or originally found in an area.

Organism   A living thing such as an animal or plant.

Pesticide   A substance used to kill pests.

Poach   To hunt or steal something that it is against the law to kill or take.

Pollution   Something in the soil, water or air that is harmful to plants and animals.

Reptile   A cold-blooded animal with a backbone, such as a snake or lizard. Reptiles are often covered in scales.

Restoration   Returning something to the way it used to be.

Sewage   Dirty water from toilets and drains.

Species   A group of plants and animals that are very similar and can breed with each other.

Sustainable   Something that we can carry on using or doing for a long time without it being used up.

Vegetation   Plant life.

Try searching for these online to find more ways you can help:

Go ladybird spotting with the UK Ladybird Survey

Hunt for sexton beetles with the National Silphidae Recording Scheme

Look out for oil beetles with Buglife

Watch out for weevils with the Weevil Recording Scheme

Look out for longhorn beetles with the Longhorn Recording Scheme

Hunt for grasshoppers with the Grasshopper and Related Species Recording Scheme

Sniff out dung beetles with DUMP! (the dung beetle UK mapping project)

Create a buzz with the Great British Bee Count

Index